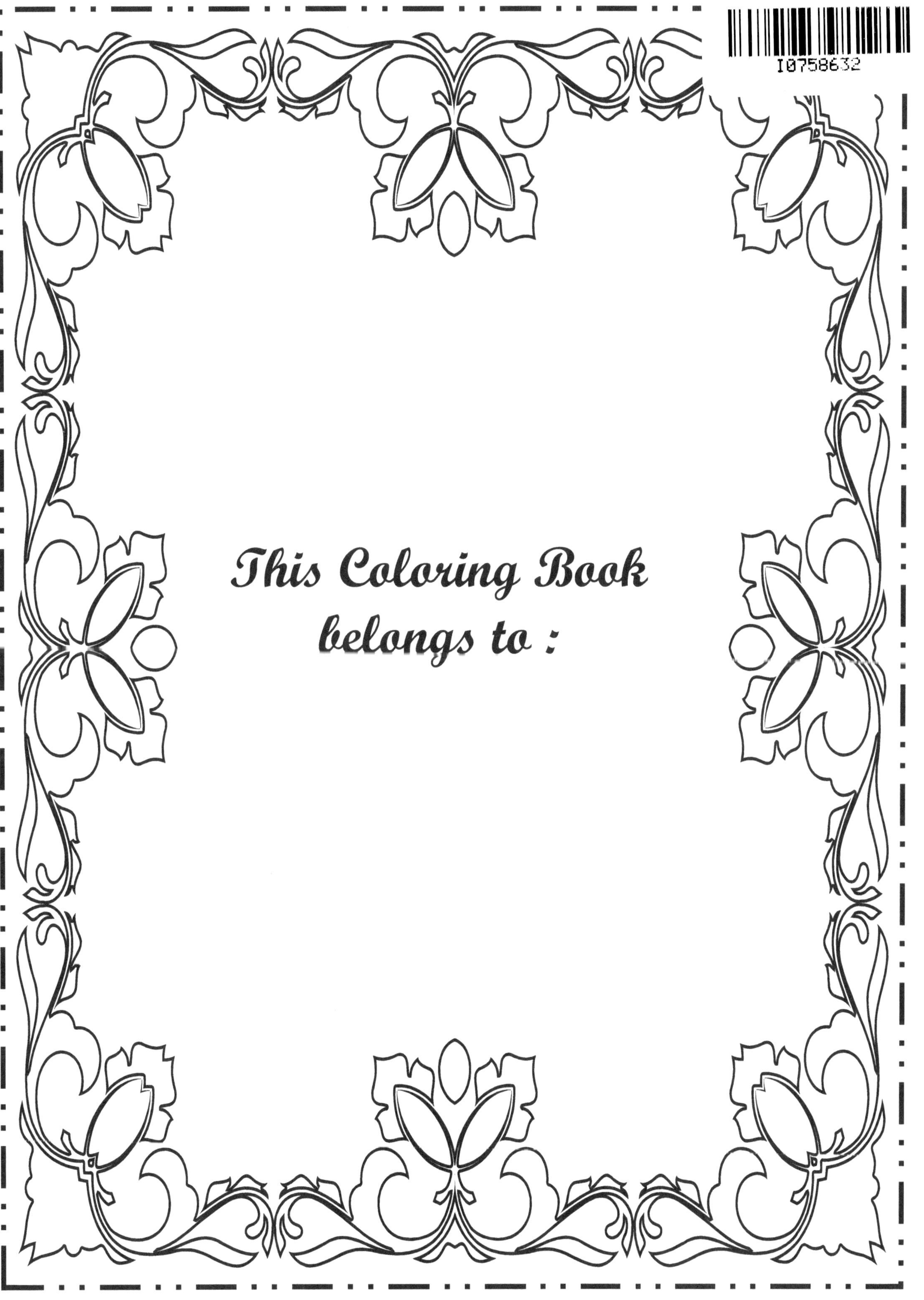
This Coloring Book
belongs to :

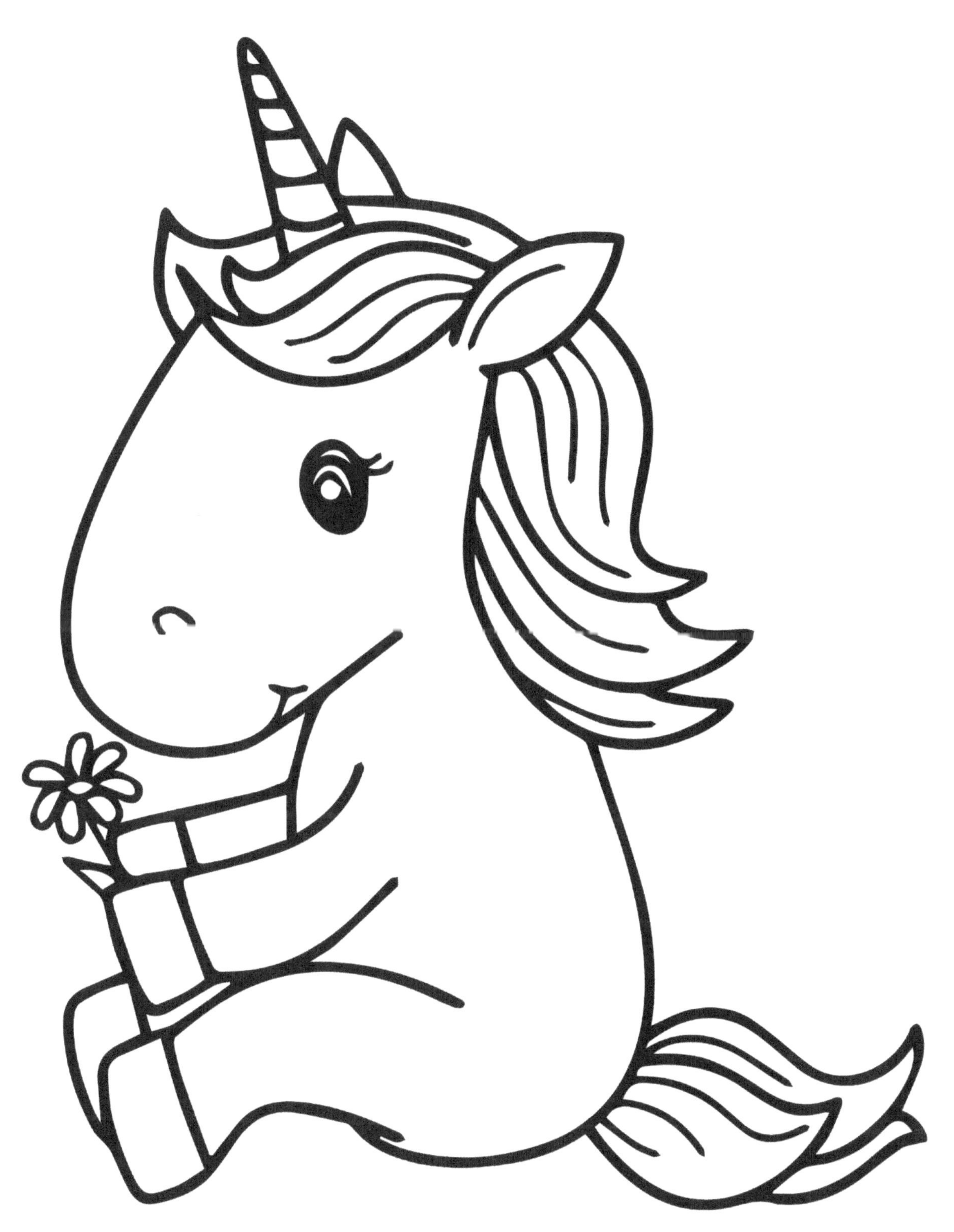

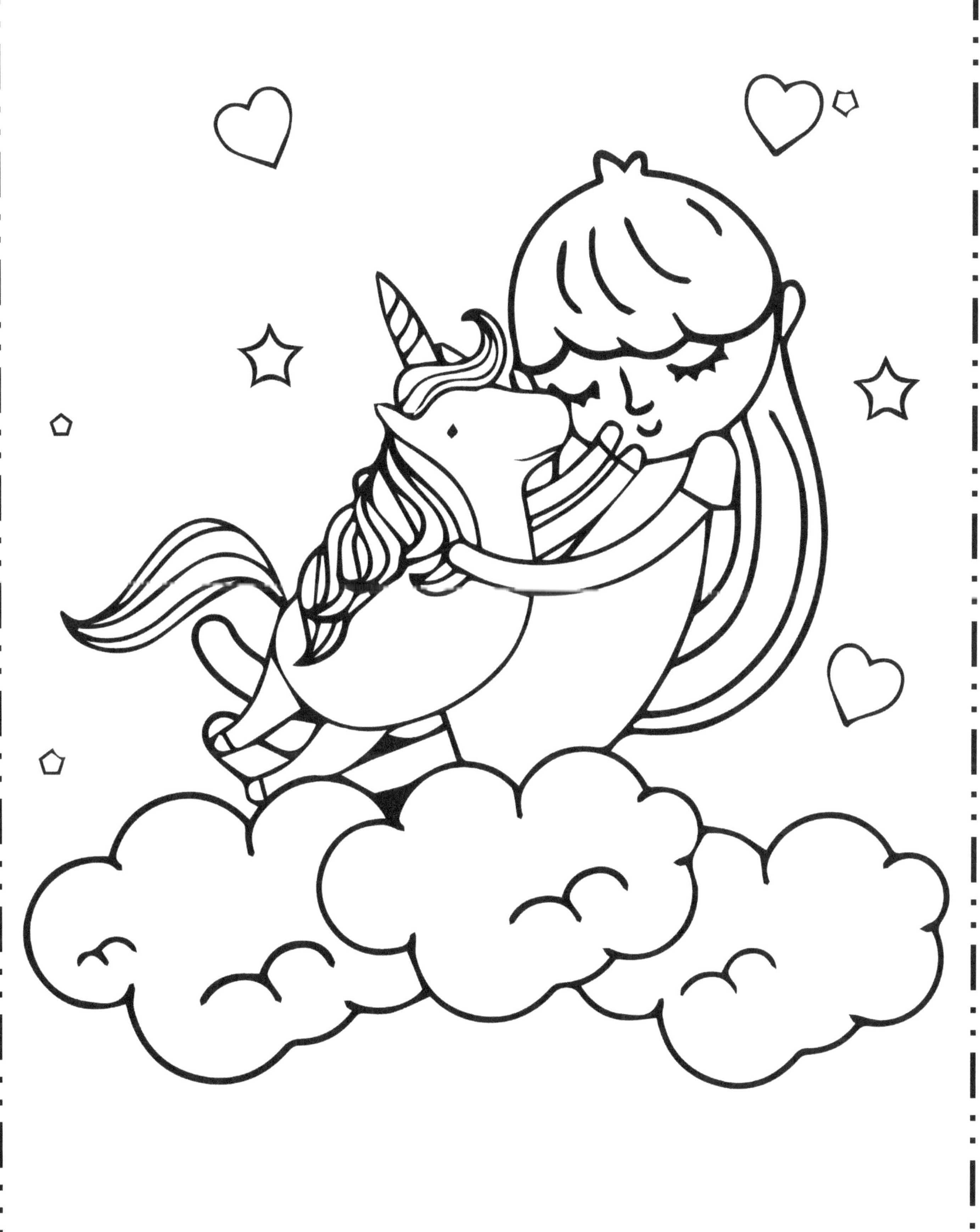

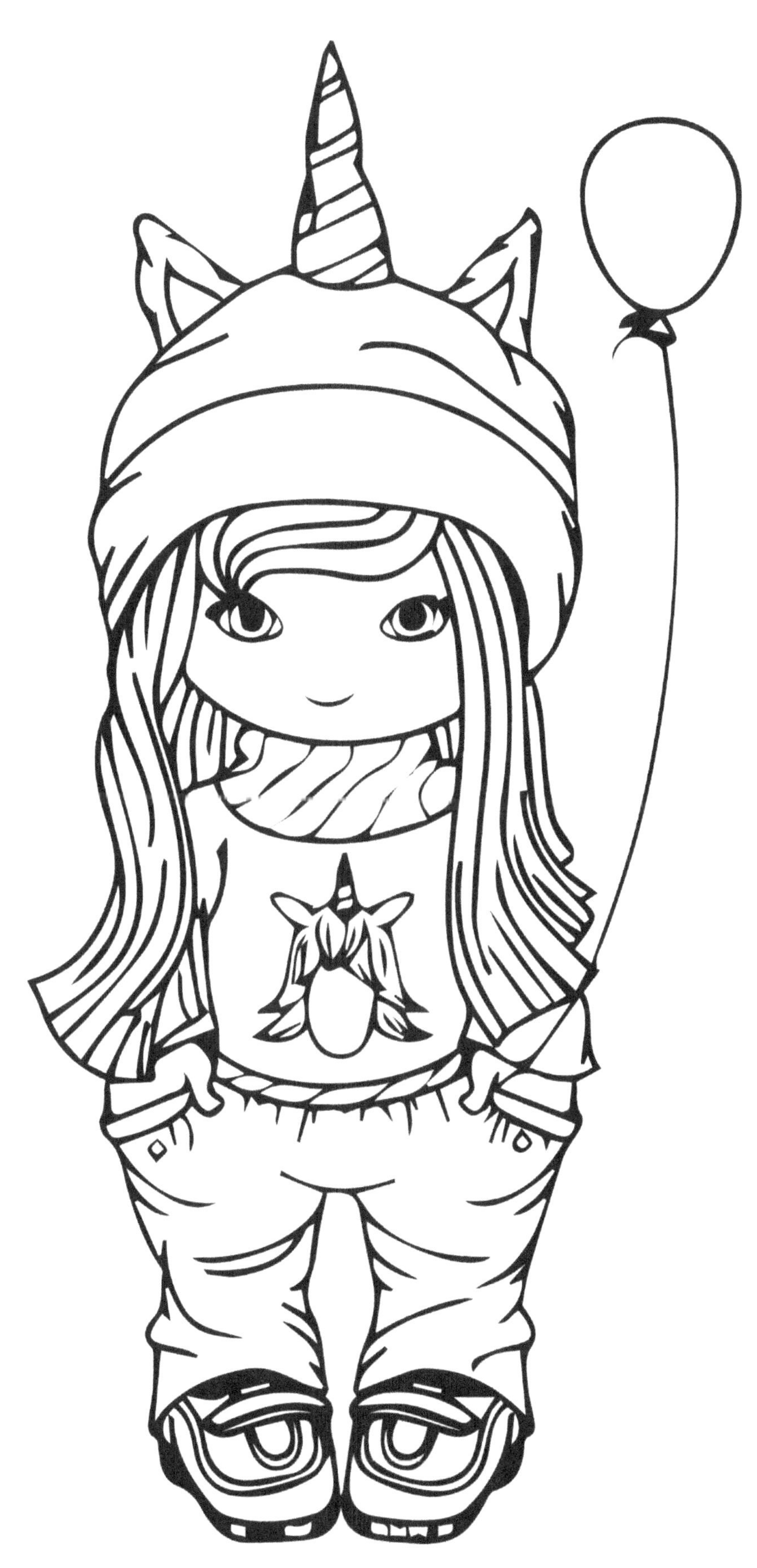

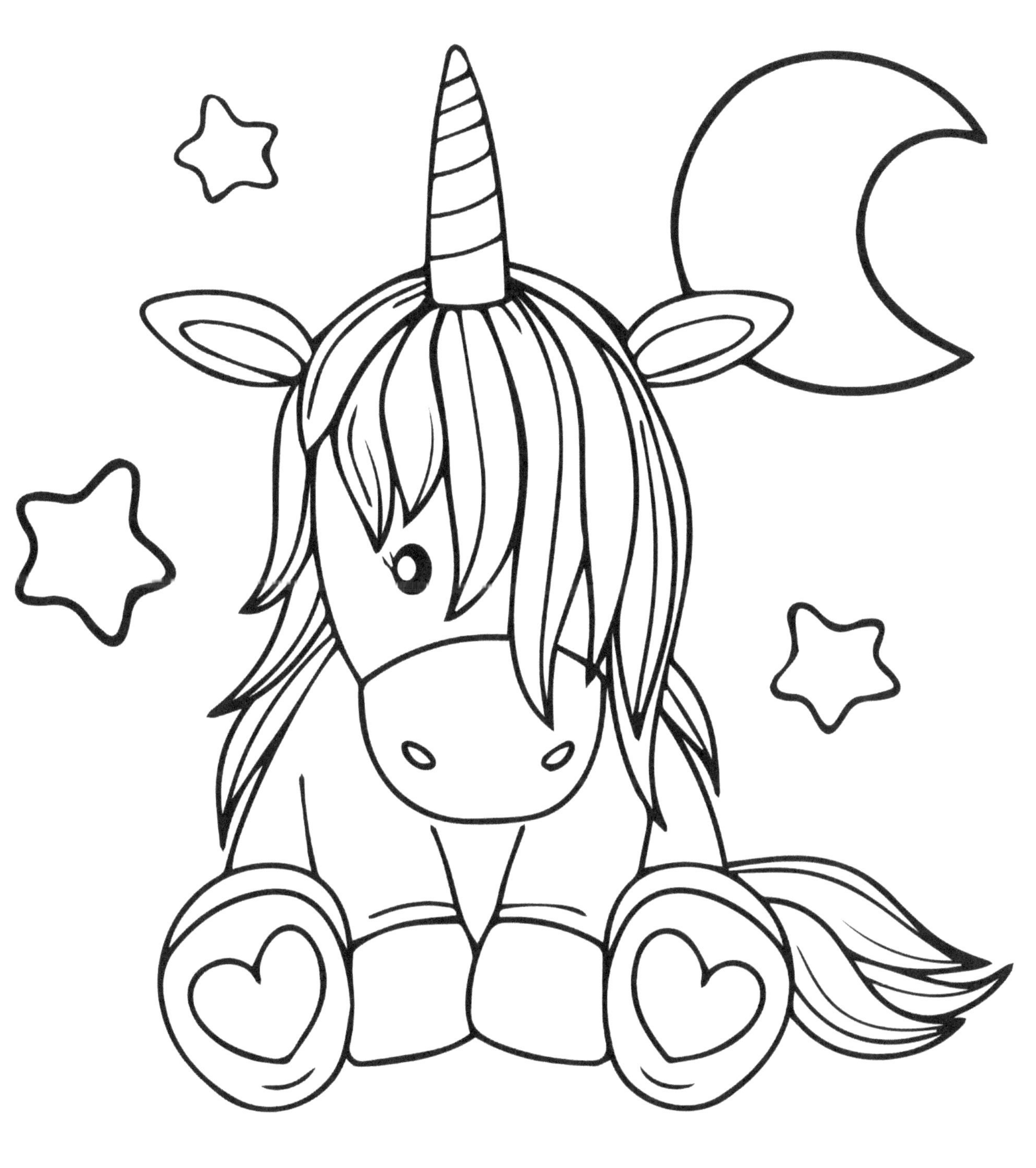

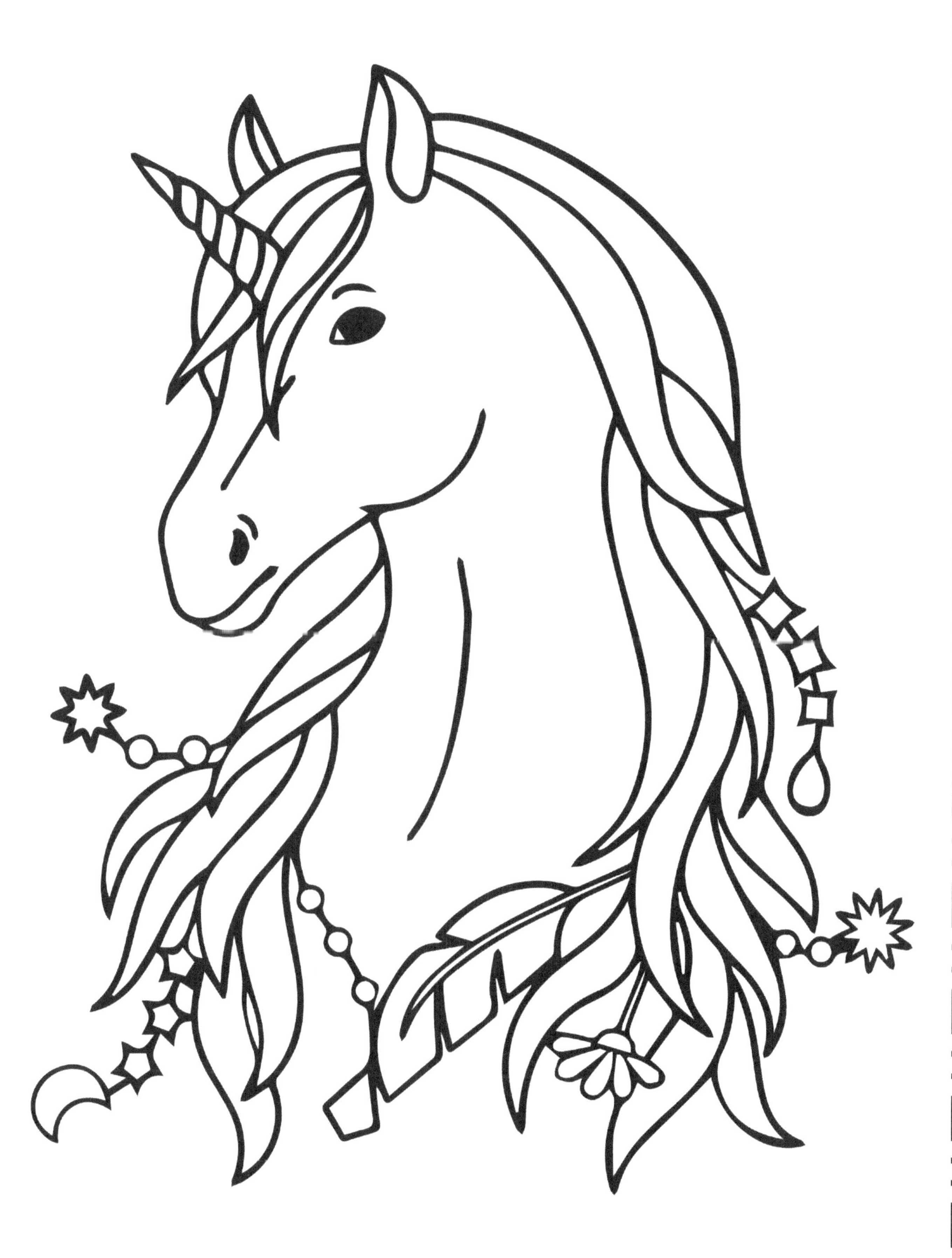

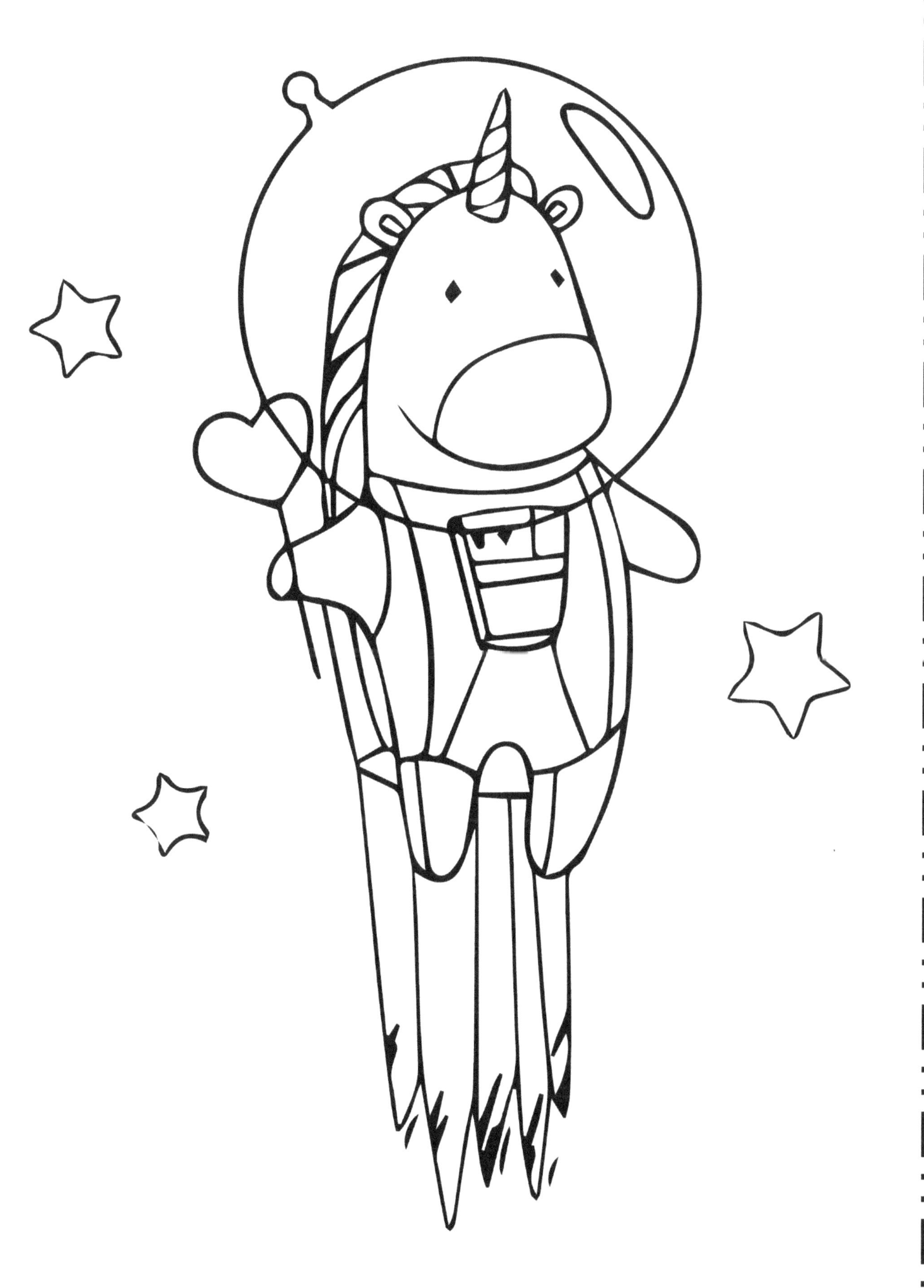

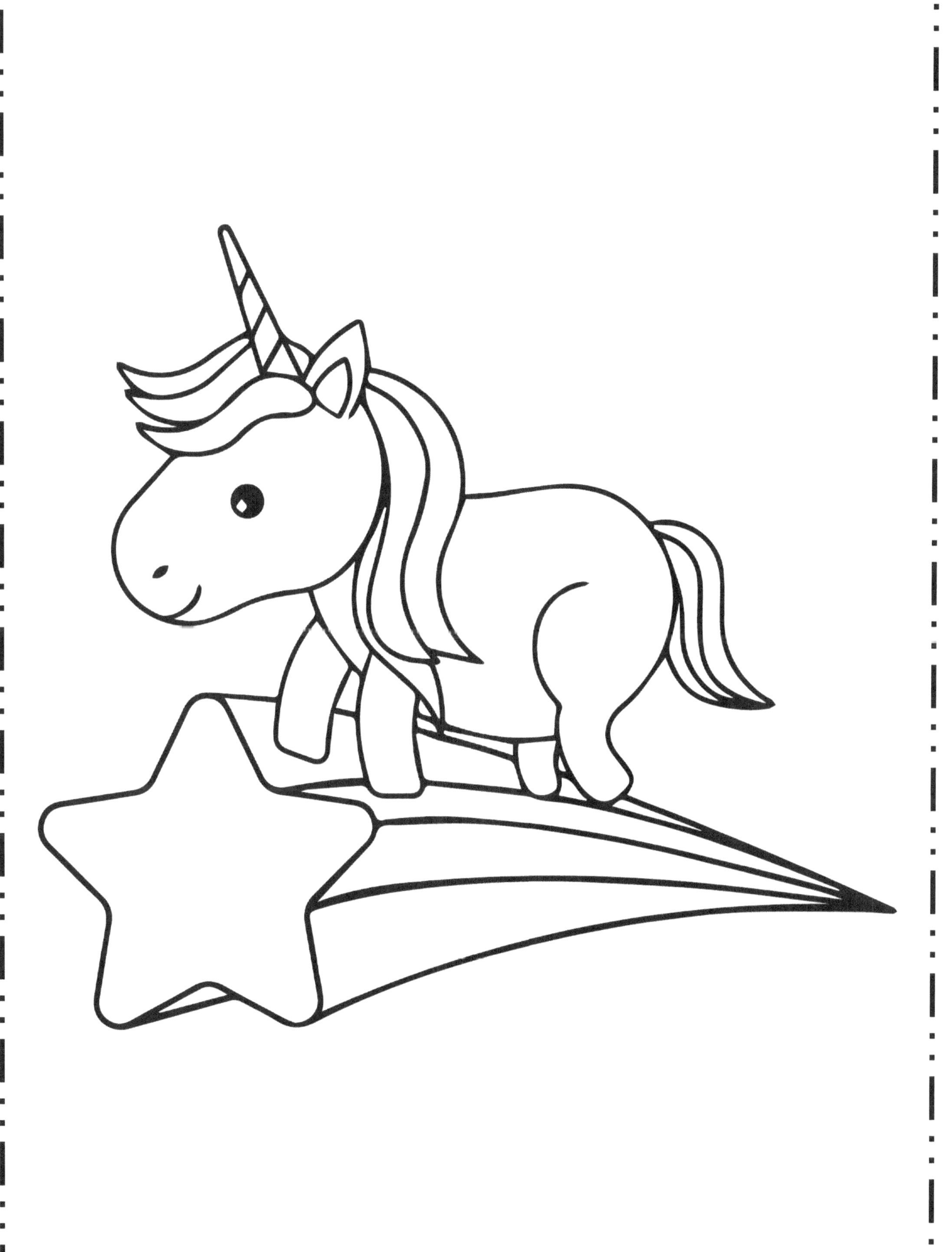

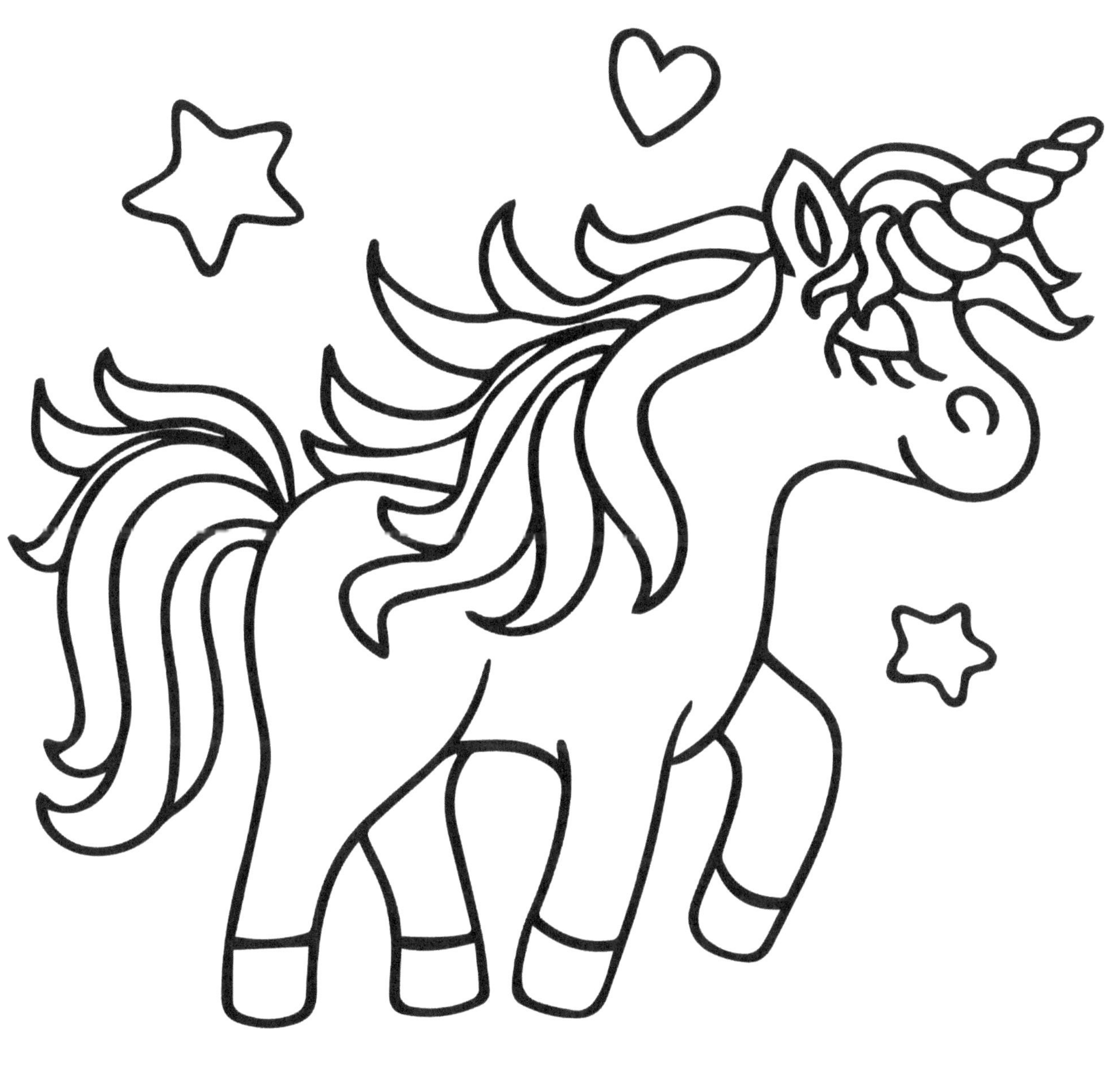

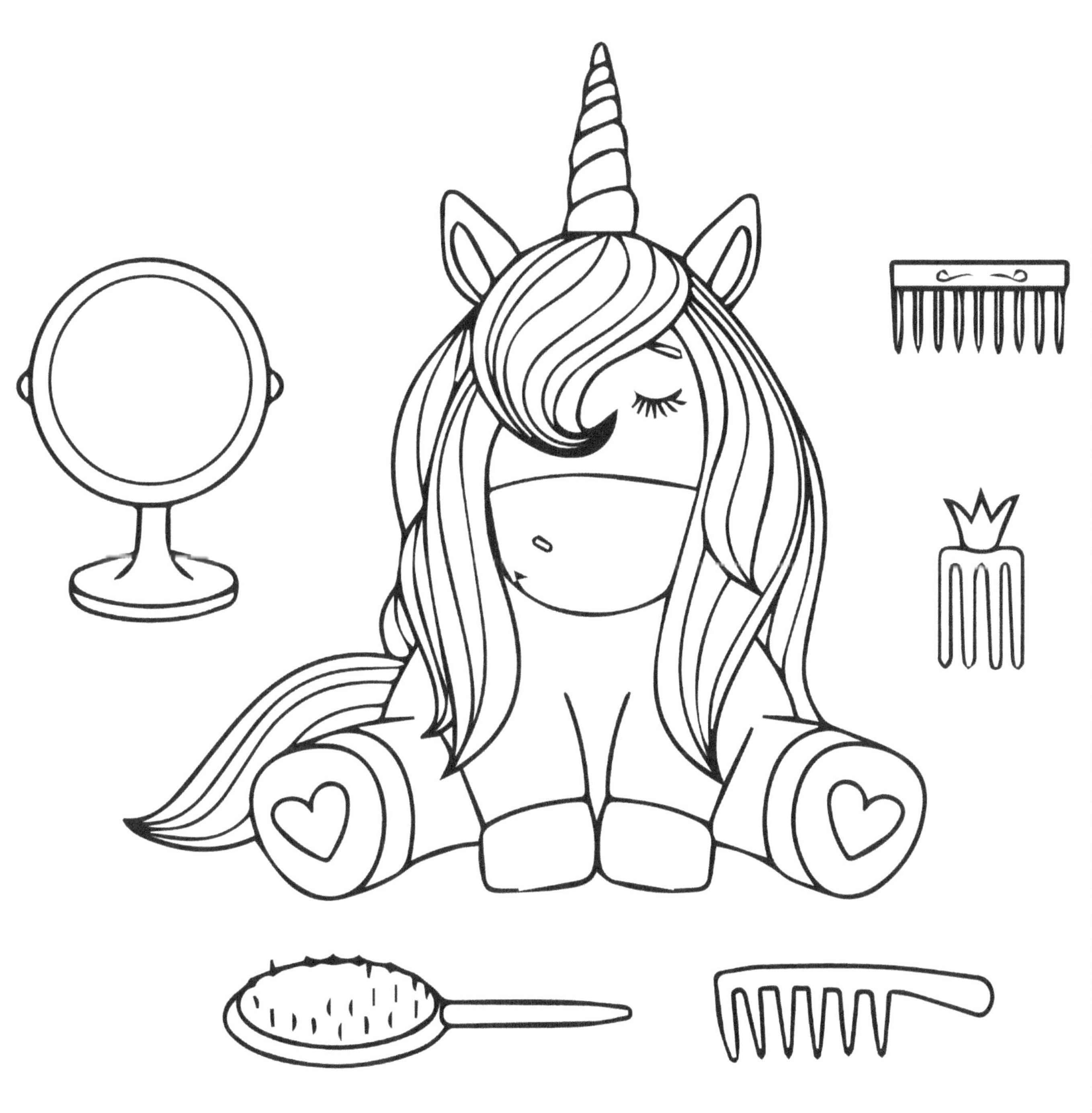

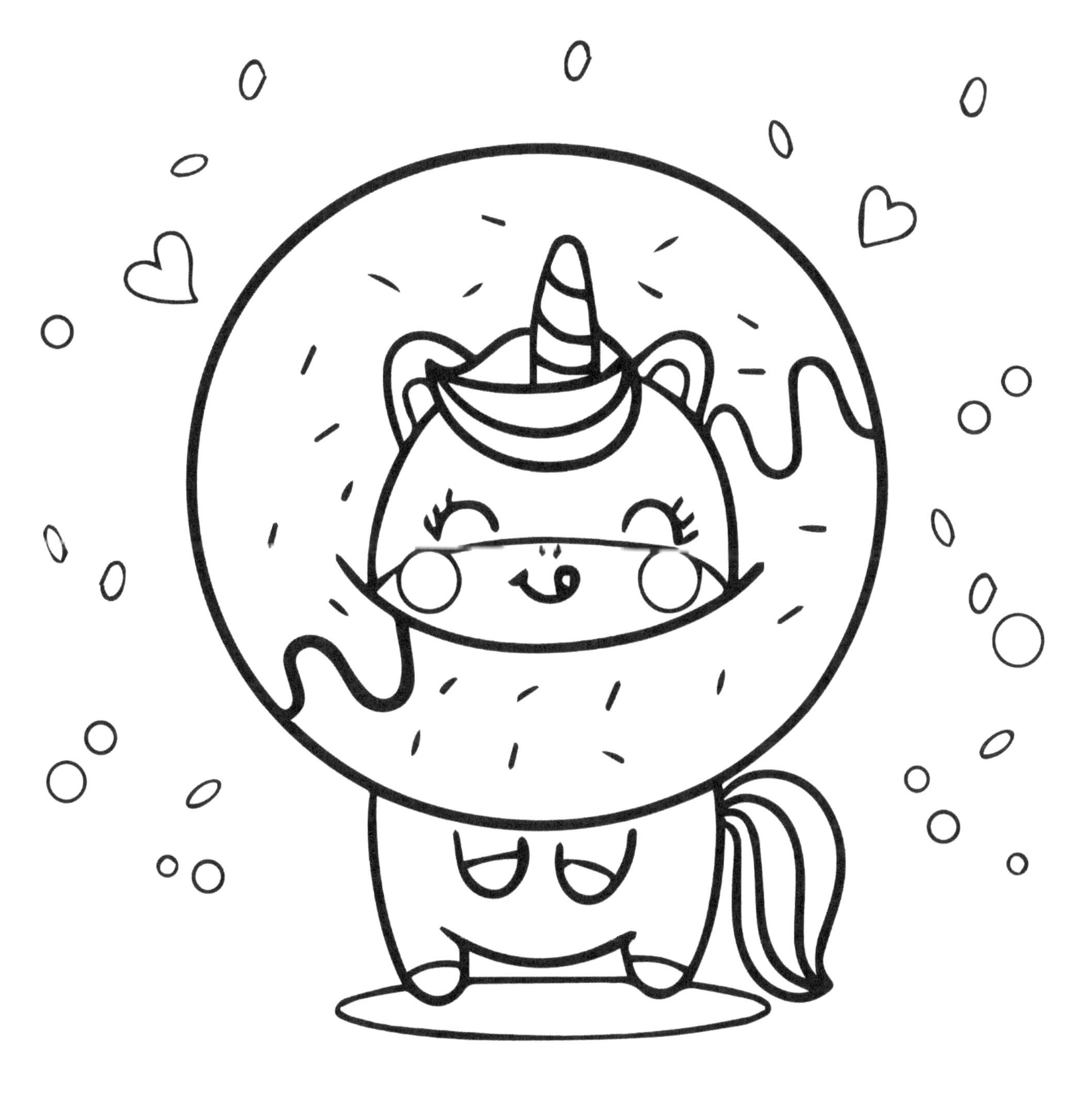

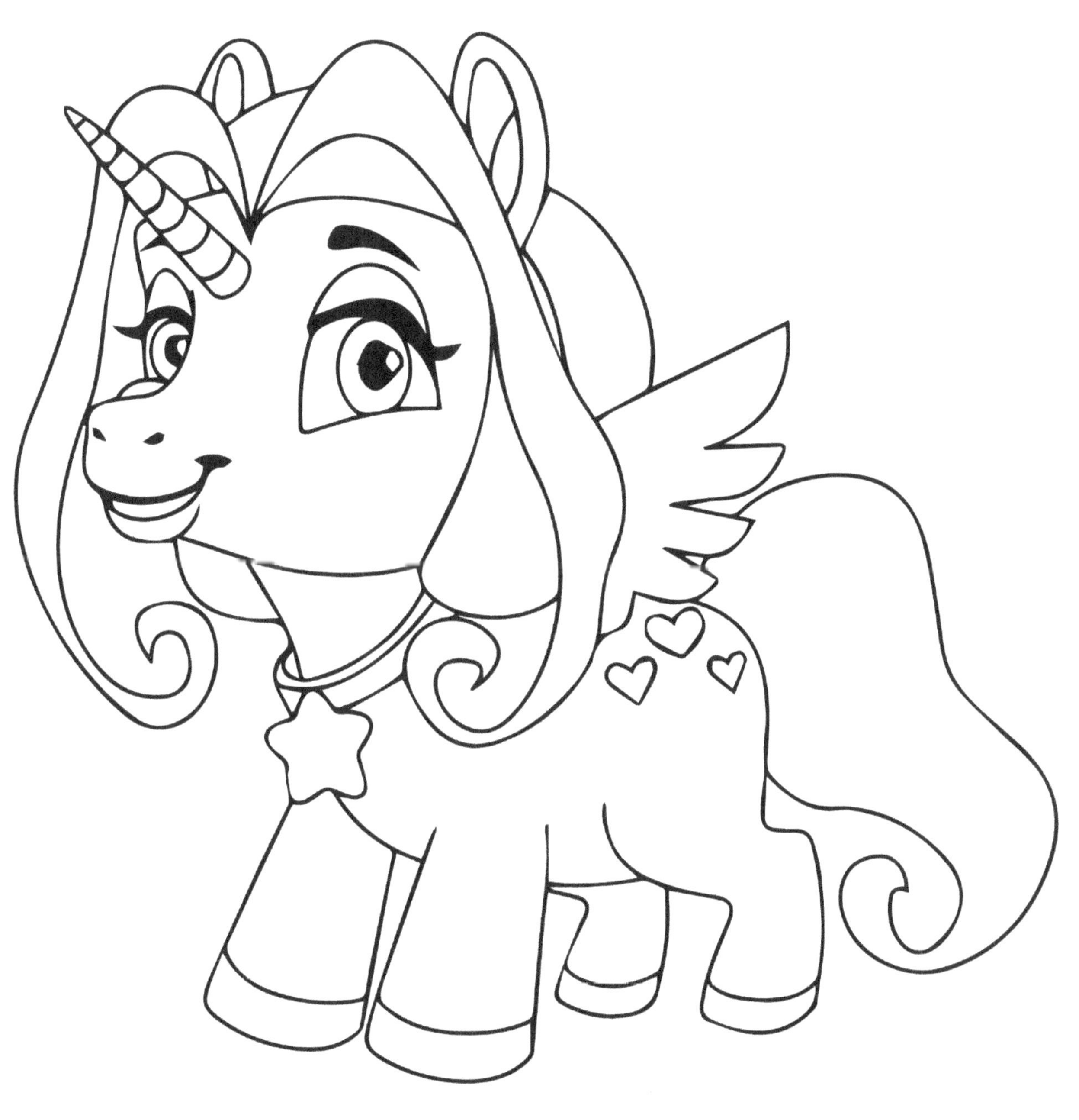

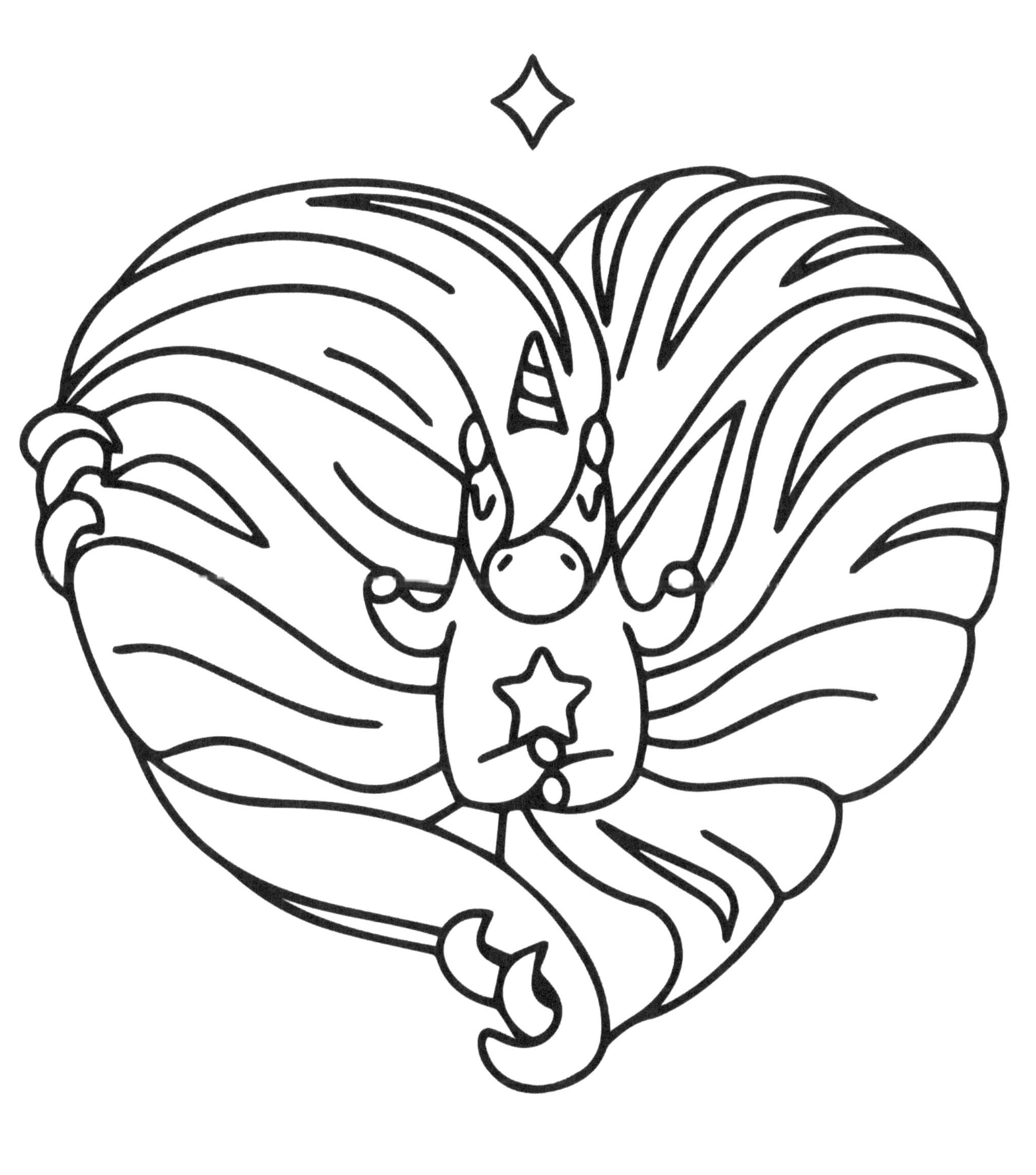

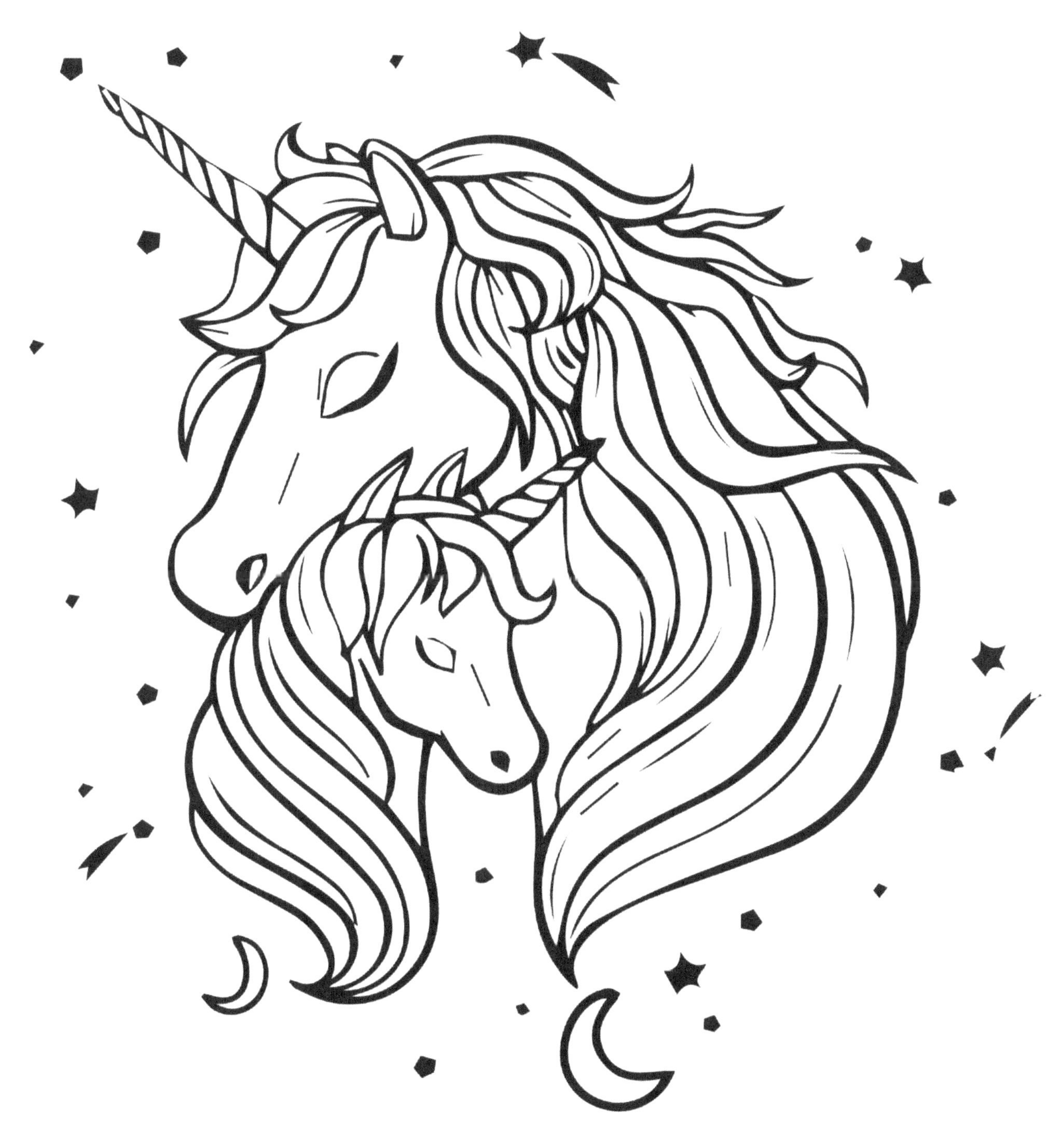

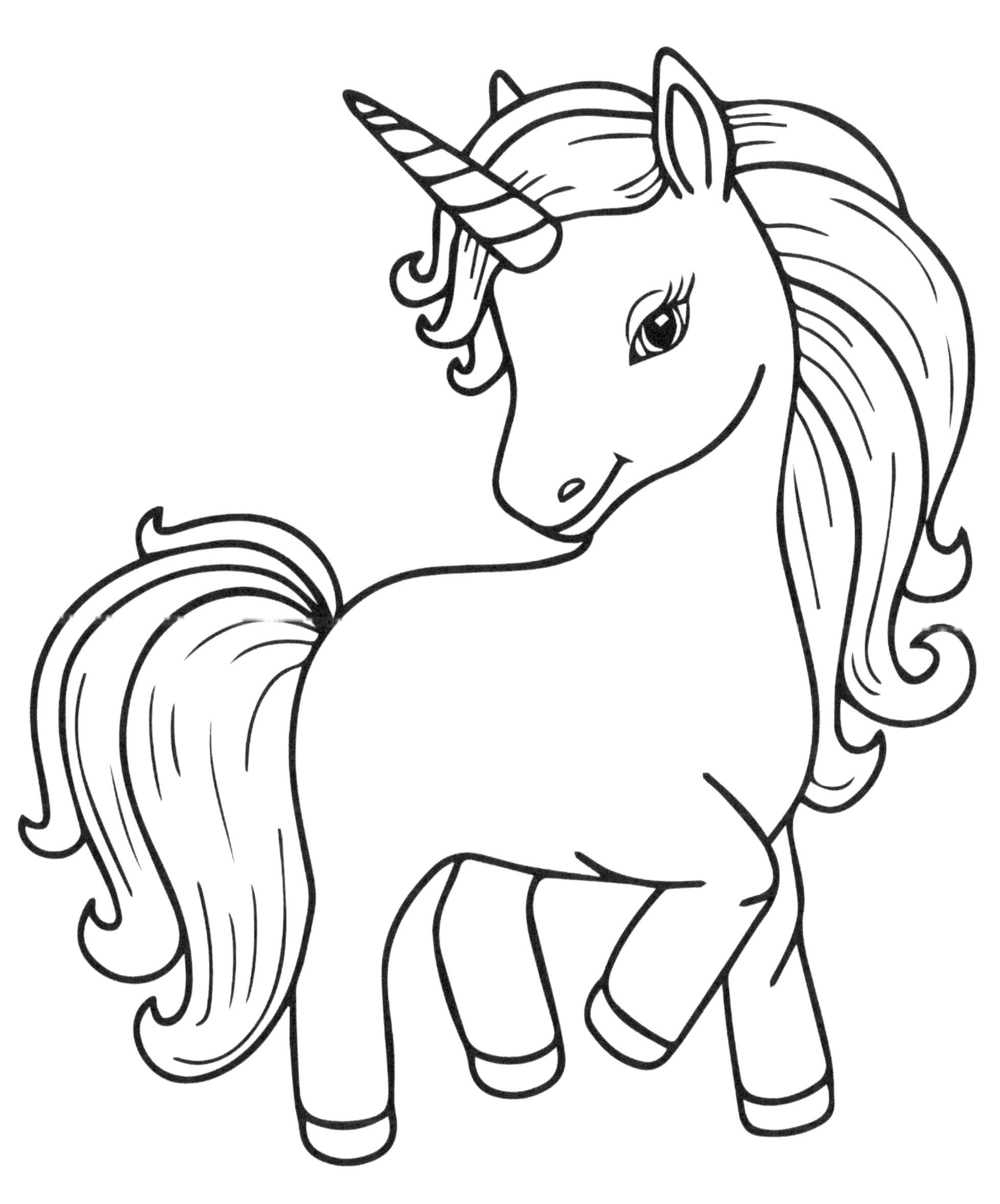

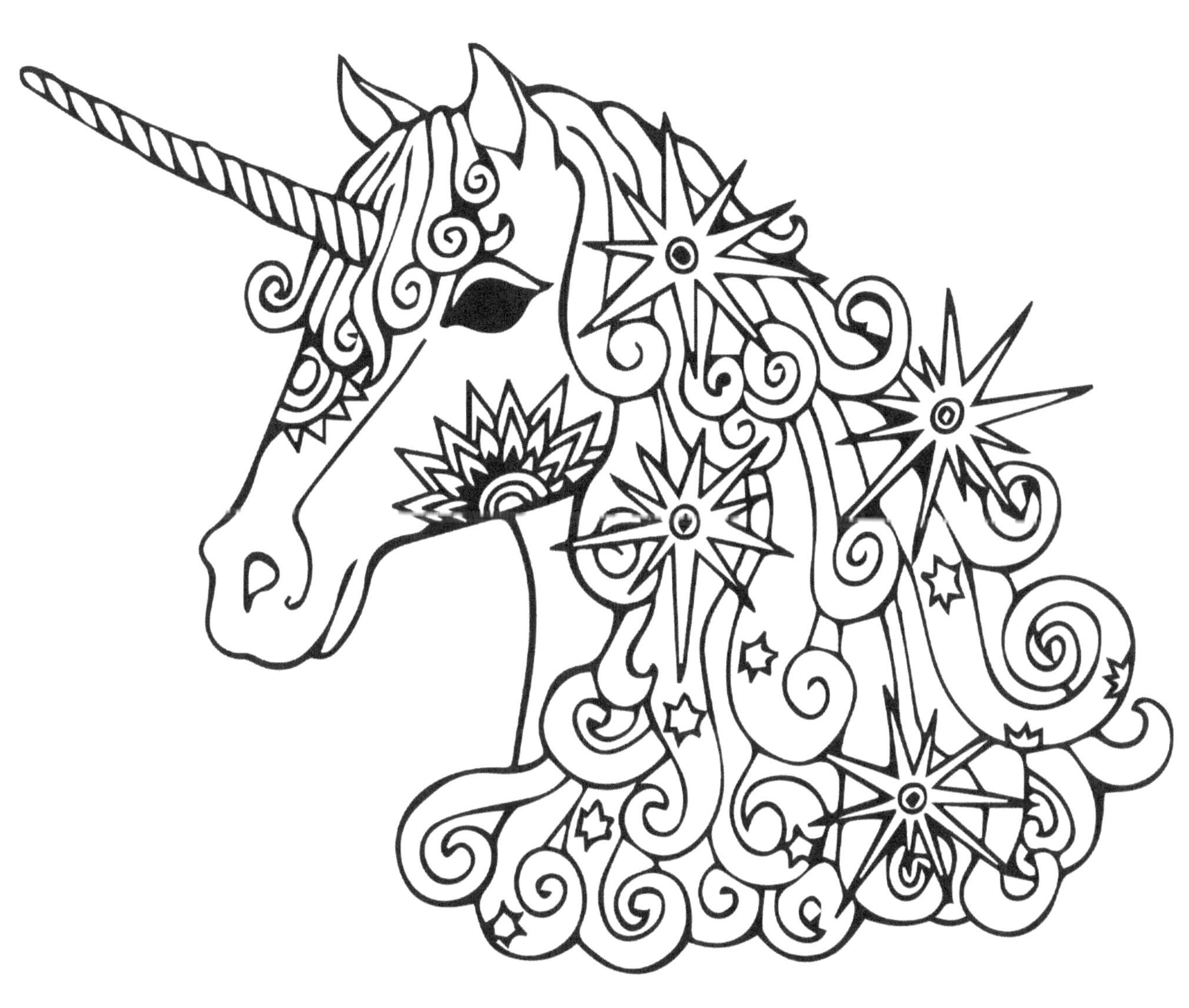

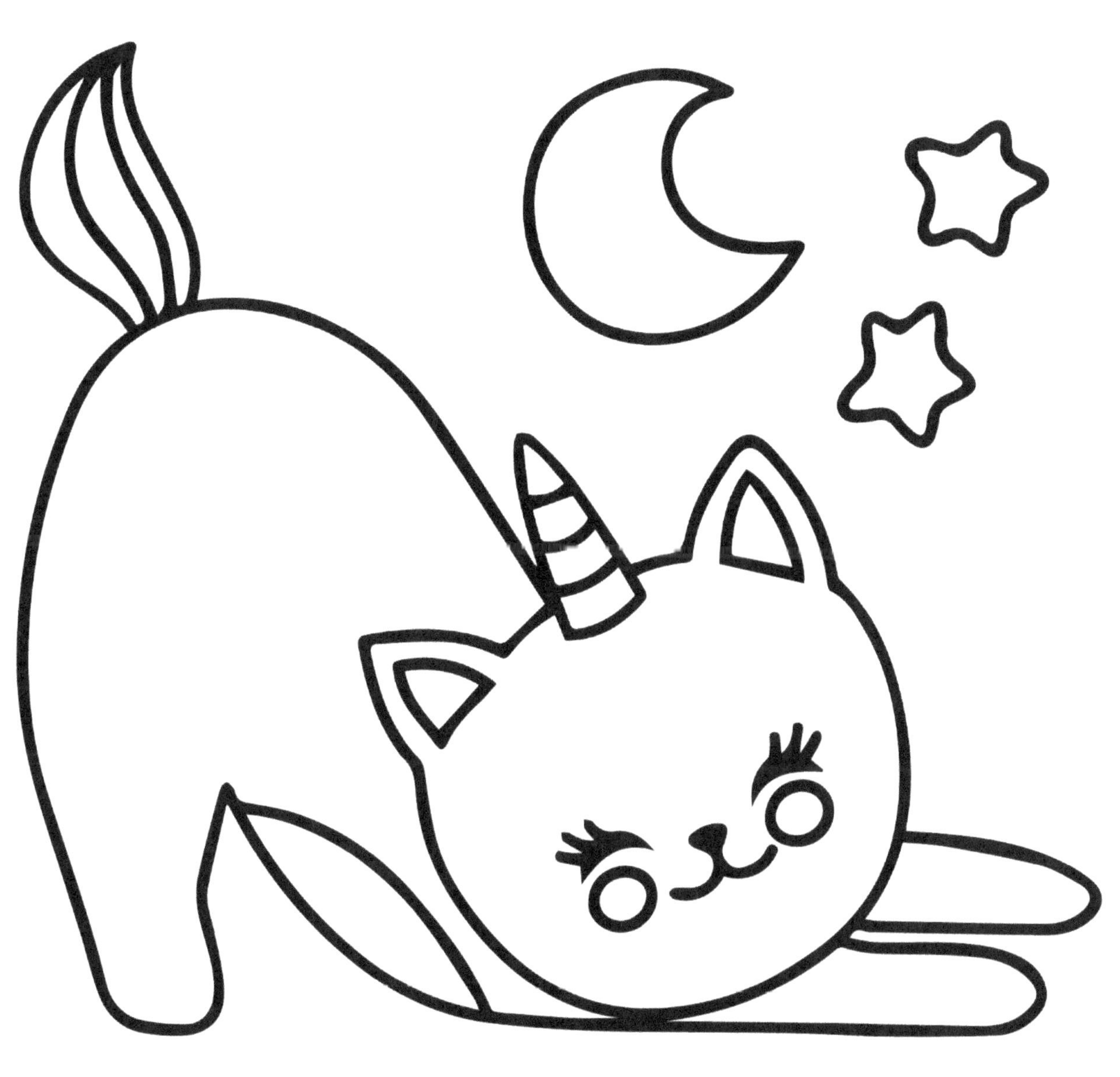

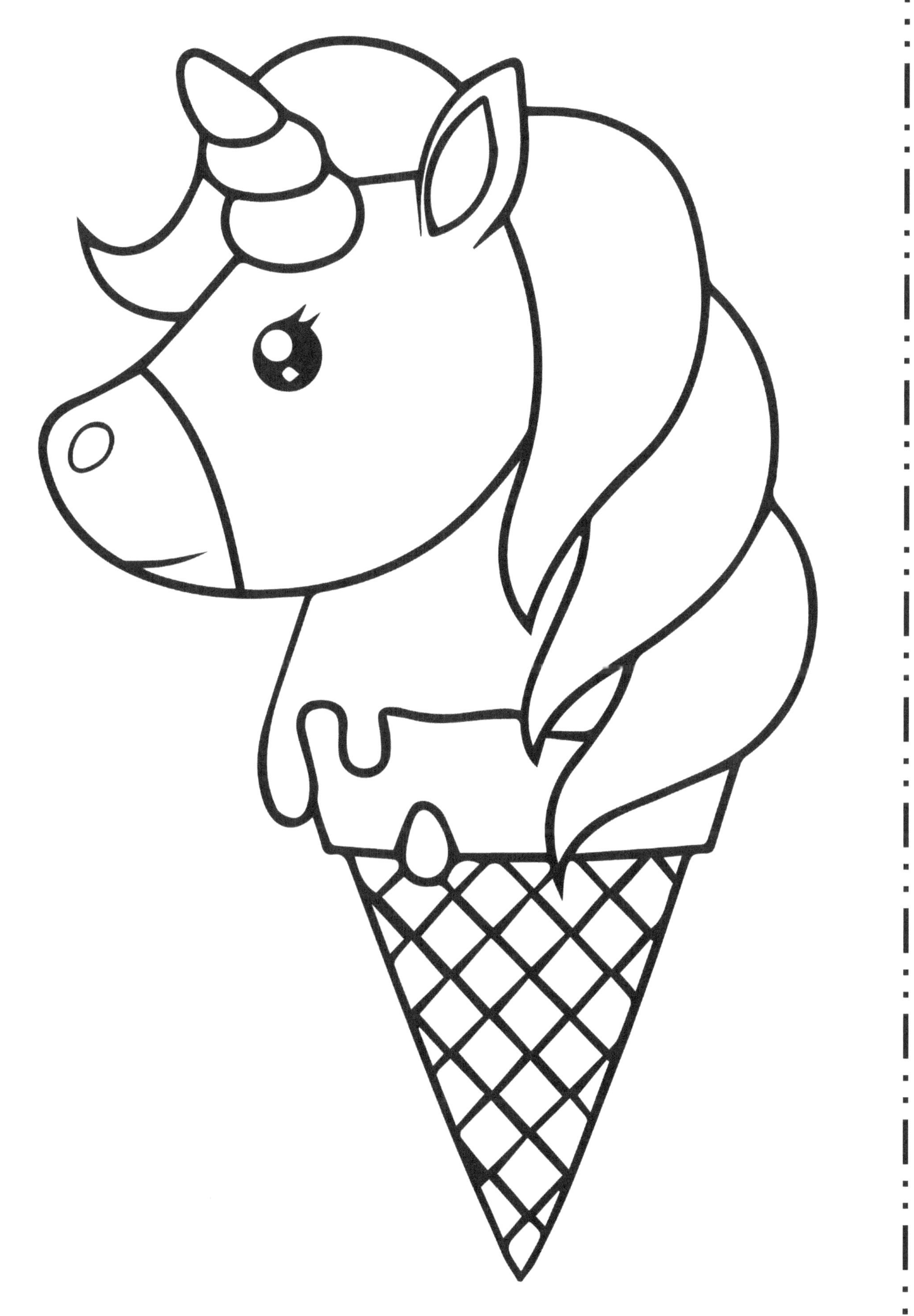

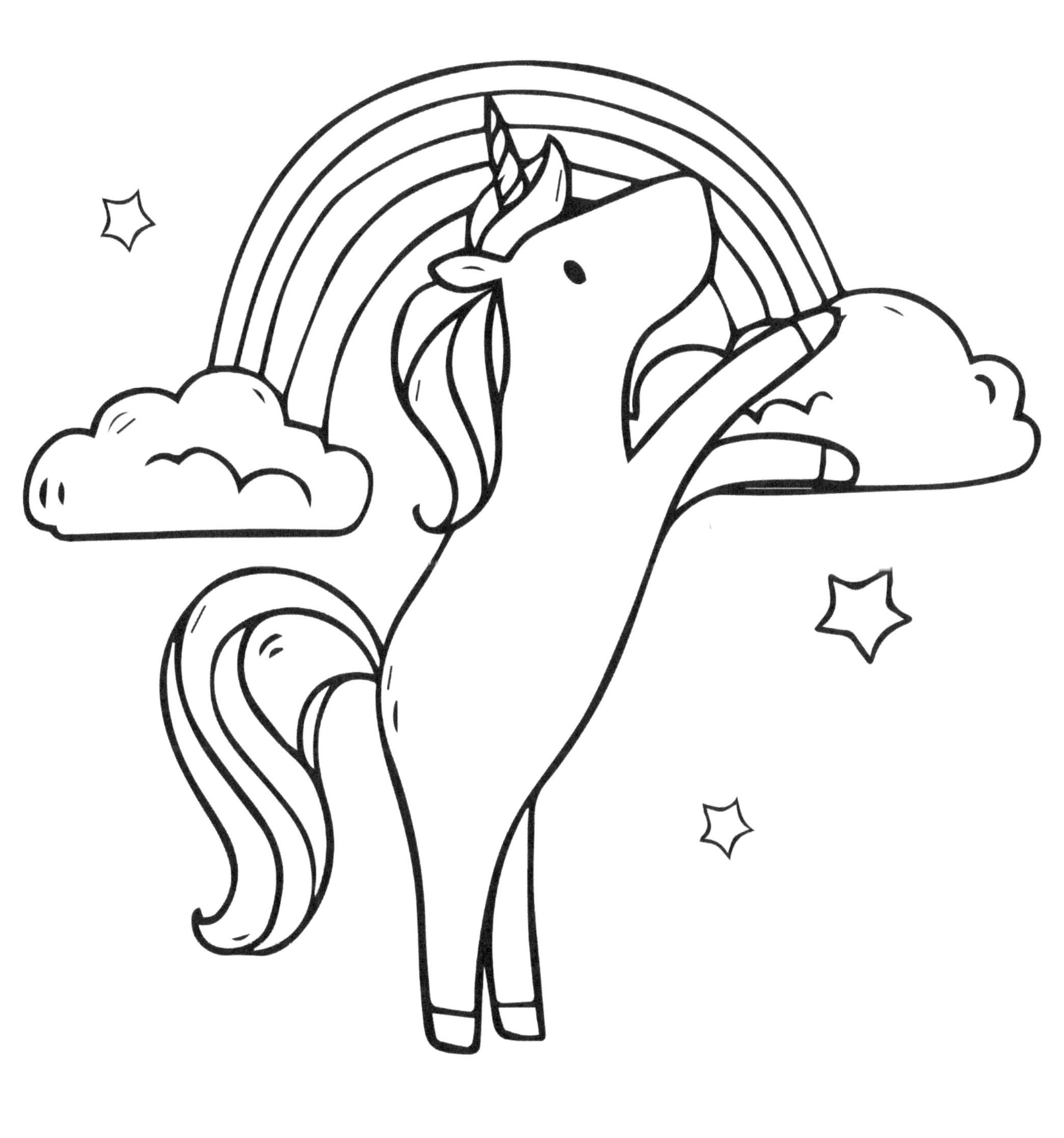

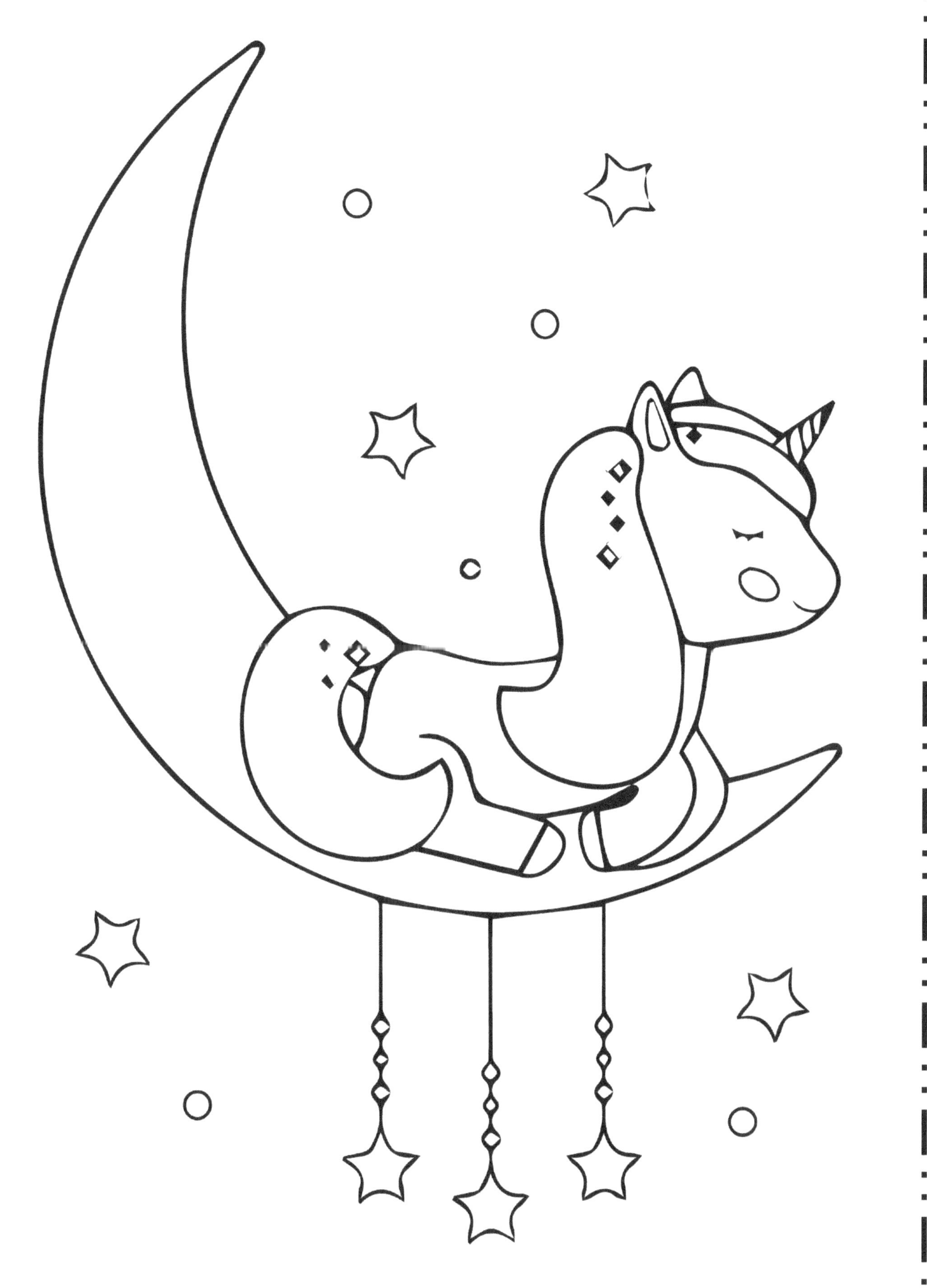

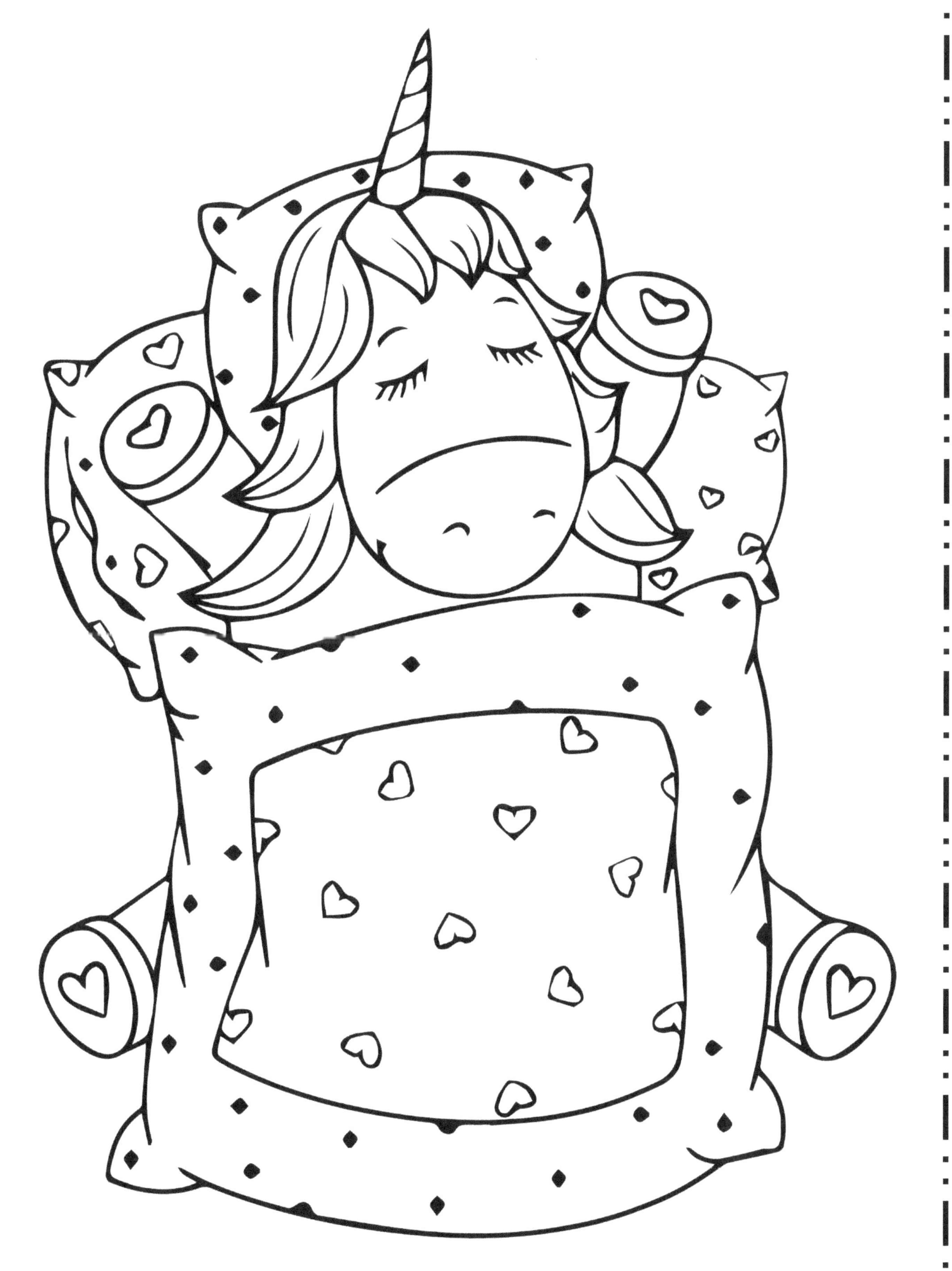

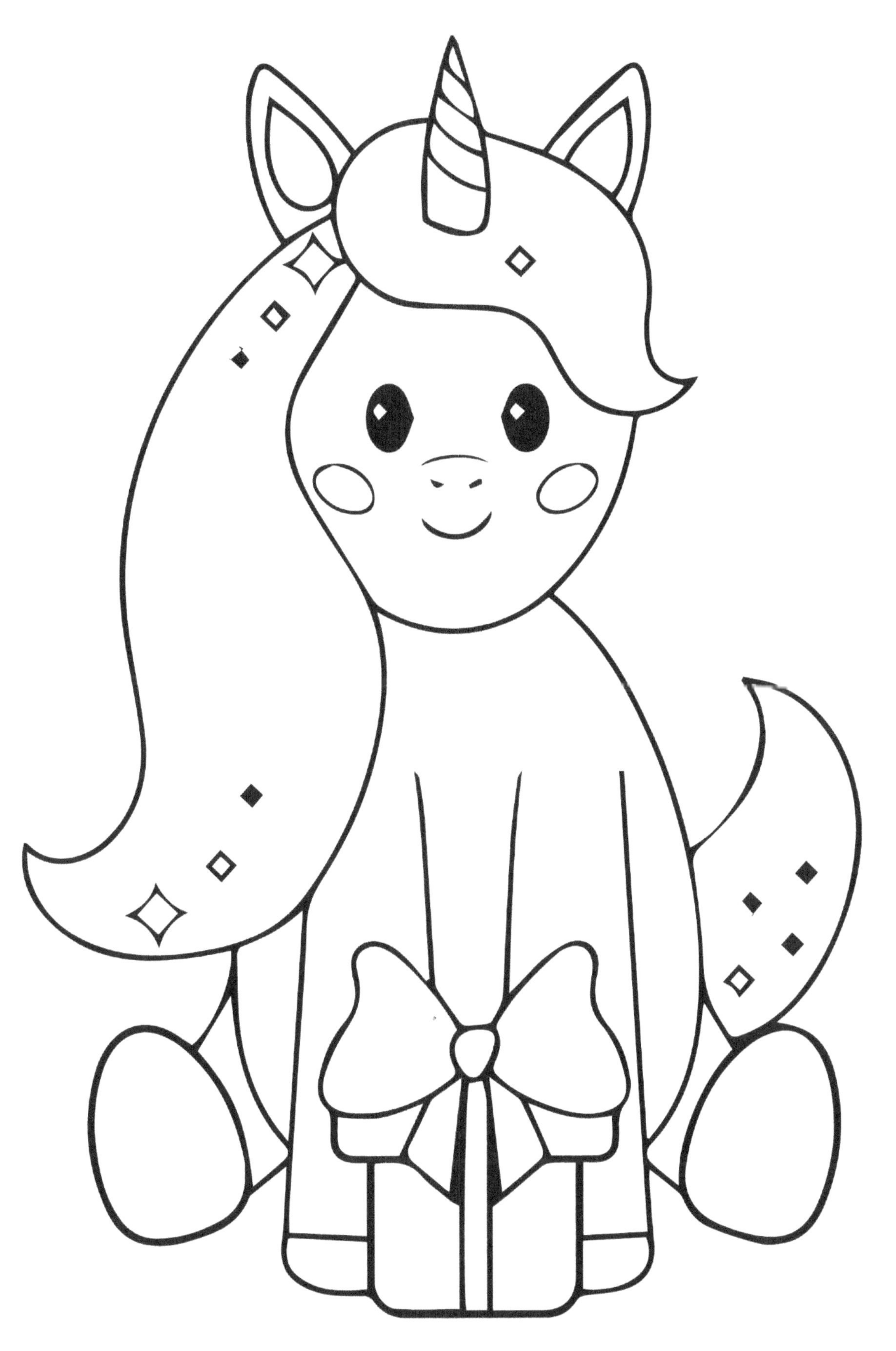

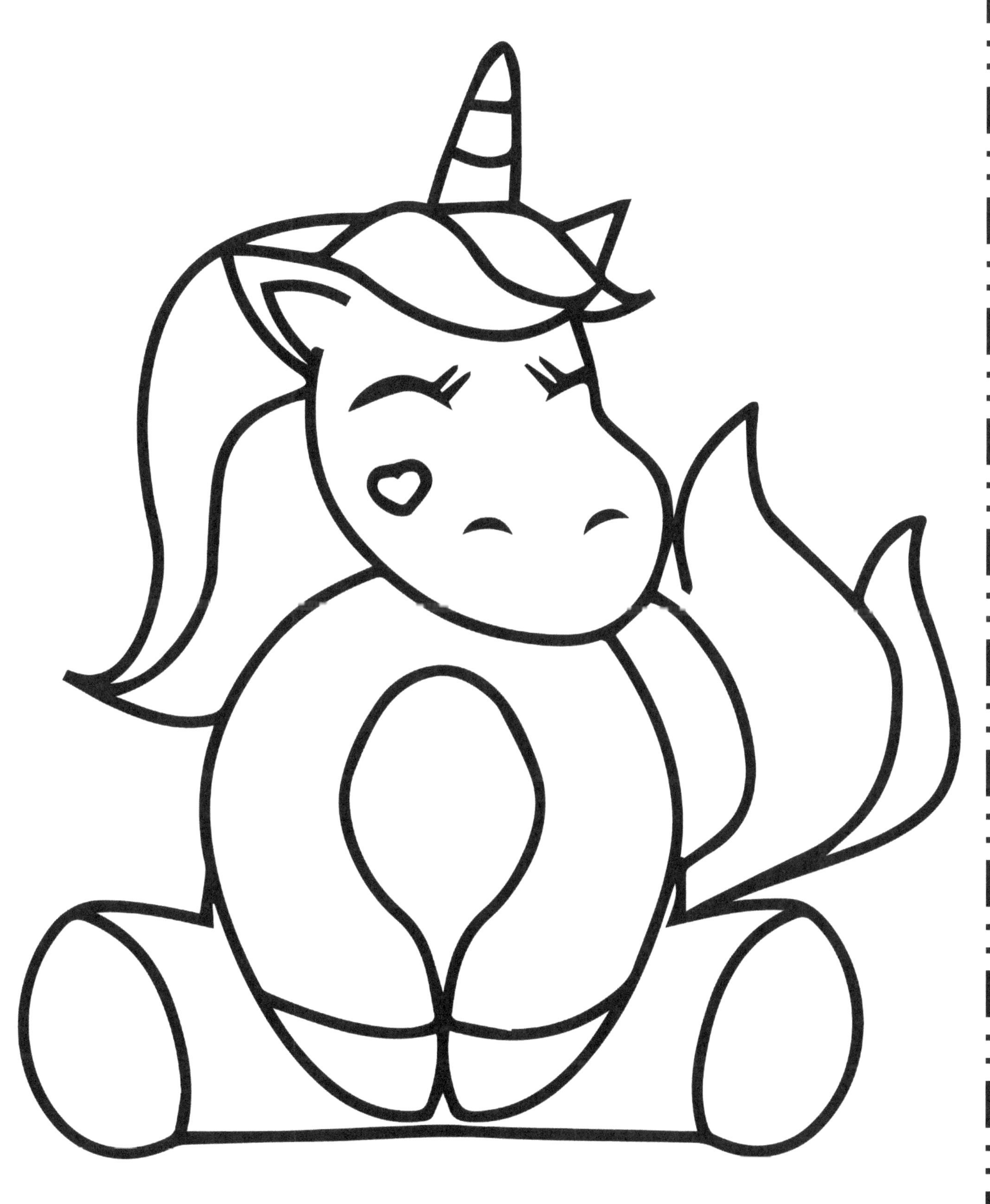

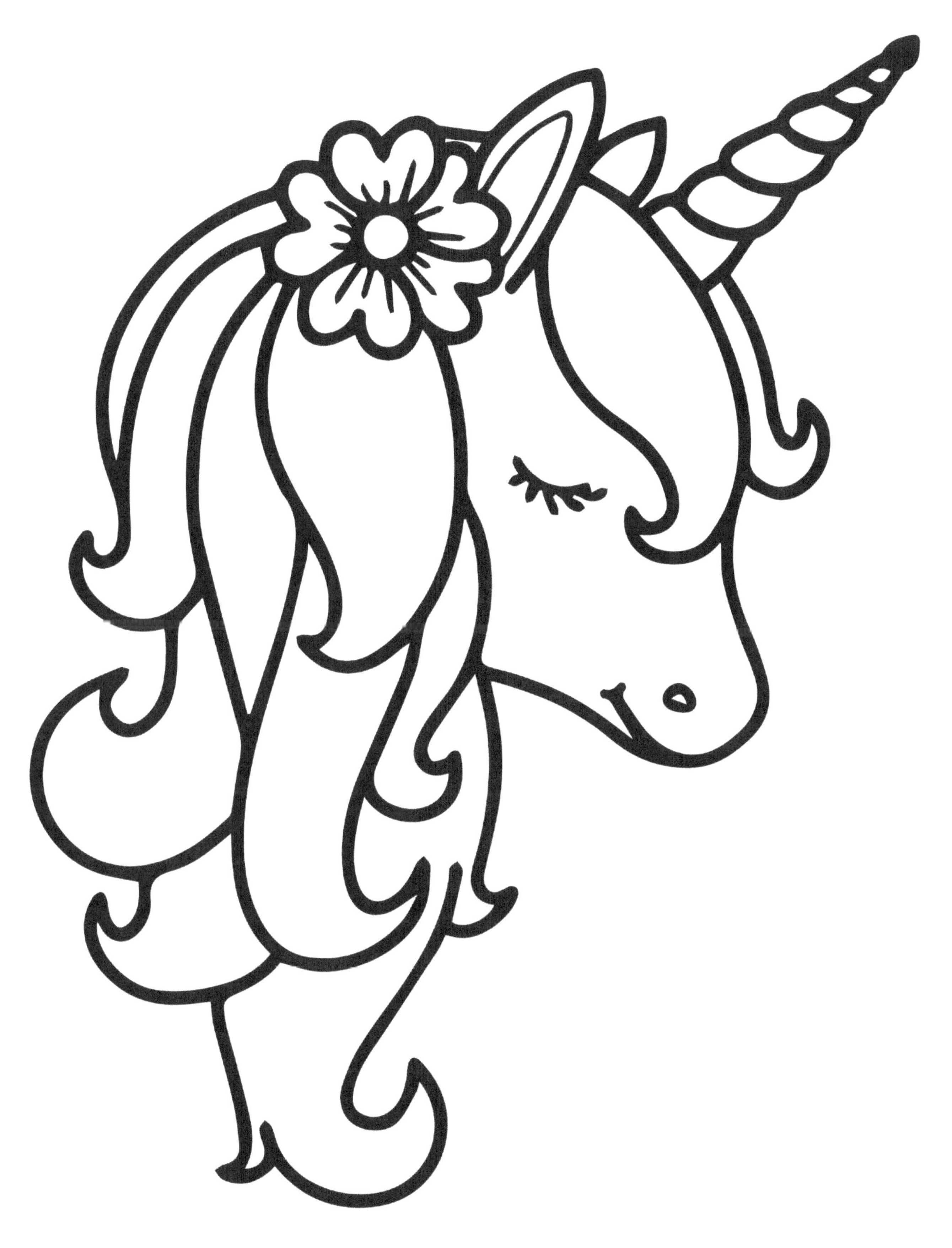

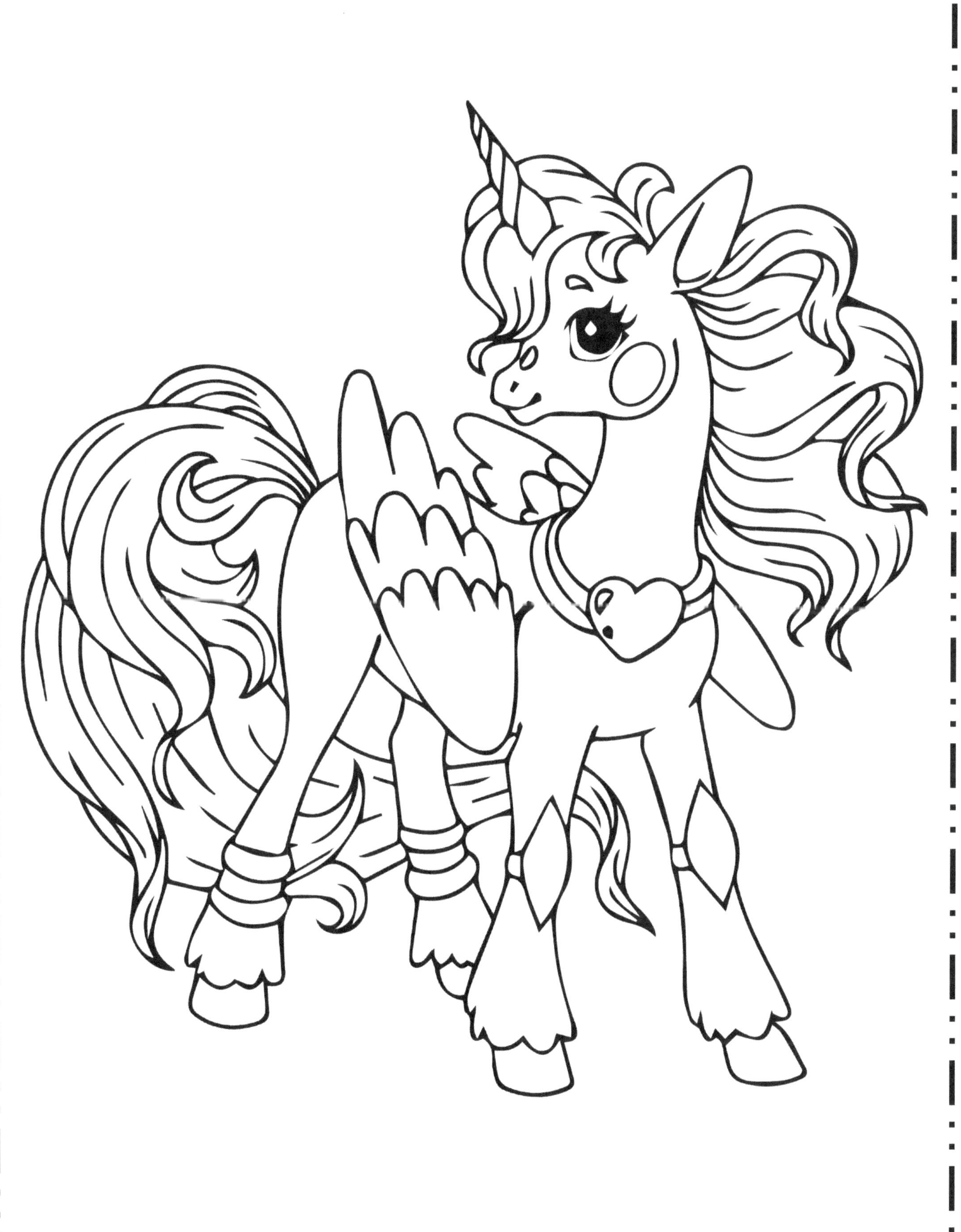

www.ingramcontent.com/pod-product-compliance
Lightning Source LLC
Chambersburg PA
CBHW080243260726
48658CB00008B/3219

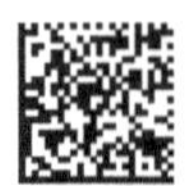
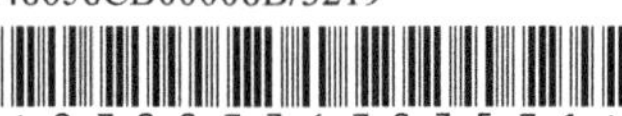